THE EMAIL ADVANTAGE

The Email Advantage

Maximizing Your Marketing Potential with Effective Email Campaigns

B. VINCENT

RWG Publishing

Contents

Chapter 1

Chapter 1: The Power of Email Marketing: An Introduction to The Email Advantage

In this day and age of digital technology, email marketing has emerged as one of the most effective methods for companies to engage with their target audience, raise the profile of their brand, and generate sales. Email marketing is a cost-effective and efficient way to reach a large audience, according to a study that was conducted by The Radicati Group. Given that the number of global email users is expected to reach 4.3 billion by the year 2023, this statistic indicates that email marketing will continue to grow in popularity.

The ability to use email marketing as a tool to maximize your marketing potential is what we mean when we talk about having the email advantage. This book was written with the intention of assisting business owners and marketers in maximizing the potential of email marketing to grow their companies and boost their revenues. The purpose of this chapter is to serve as an introduction to the book by providing an overview of the numerous advantages of email marketing and laying the groundwork for the chapters that will follow.

The Advantages of Utilizing Email Marketing

Email marketing provides a variety of benefits that are applicable to companies of varying sizes. The following is a list of the most important advantages:

Email marketing is one of the most cost-effective forms of digital marketing, making it one of the most popular as well. It makes it possible for companies to communicate with a large number of people without having to spend a lot of money on advertising.

Reach: The number of people who use email is expected to reach 4.3 billion by the year 2023, which means that email marketing offers businesses an enormous reach for connecting with the audience they are trying to reach.

Personalization: Businesses can tailor their message

and offer to a subscriber's specific interests, behavior, and preferences through the use of email marketing, which enables this feature.

Analytics: Email marketing platforms provide comprehensive analytics that enable businesses to monitor the efficacy of their marketing campaigns, locate areas in which they can make improvements, and tweak those marketing campaigns so that they produce better results.

Automation: Email automation enables businesses to save time and resources by setting up targeted marketing campaigns that are activated in response to particular actions or behaviors of their customers.

Conversion: Research has shown that email marketing has a high conversion rate. This is due to the fact that subscribers are more likely to act when they are presented with an offer or call-to-action in an email.

Putting the Pieces Together for a Profitable Email Marketing Campaign

It is essential to have a strong foundation in place before beginning a marketing campaign via email. The following are the most important aspects to consider when developing a successful strategy for email marketing:

Your email marketing campaigns should have crystal-clear and measurable goals that you want to achieve. This could involve boosting sales, accumulating lead information, or increasing the number of visitors to your website.

Audience: Acquire an understanding of your audience in order to personalize the messaging and offers you provide in accordance with the preferences, interests, and behaviors of this group.

Email List: Develop a high-quality email list consisting of active subscribers who have opted-in to receive your emails and have subscribed to receive them.

Create content that is compelling and engaging, that speaks to your audience, and that aligns with the goals you have set for yourself.

Design: Employ a design for your email that is both eye-catching and professional, and that reflects your brand while also making it simple for subscribers to interact with your content.

Include a distinct call-to-action that encourages subscribers to take some kind of action, such as visiting your website or making a purchase, and make sure that it is as clear as possible.

Testing: To get better results from your email marketing campaigns, test and optimize them on an ongoing basis.

Conclusion

Email marketing is an effective method for companies of any size to connect with their target audience, raise the profile of their brand, and generate sales. This chapter has provided an overview of the advantages of email marketing as well as the essential components of an effective strategy for email marketing. In the following chapters, we will delve deeper into each of these components in order to assist you in optimizing your marketing potential through the use of successful email campaigns.

Chapter 2: Building Your Email List: Strategies for Capturing and Engaging Your Audience

A successful email marketing strategy will typically include a number of different components, one of the most important of which is the creation of a high-quality email list. It is essential to have a robust email list consisting of engaged subscribers who have opted-in to receive your emails in order to ensure that your message is delivered to the appropriate audience and that your campaigns are as successful as possible.

In this chapter, we will explore strategies for capturing and engaging your audience, with the end goal of building a high-quality email list that will drive engagement as well as revenue.

Develop Lead-Generating Content of a High Quality

Lead magnets are enticements of value that are provided free of charge to an audience in exchange for that audience's email address. They are an effective method for drawing in new subscribers and expanding the size of your email list. Make sure that the lead magnet you create is of a high quality, that it is relevant to your target audience, and that it provides them with something of value. In addition to this, it should be congruent with your brand and the objectives of the email marketing campaigns you run.

Make sure that your website is optimized for new signups.

By including opt-in forms on your website, you will make it simple for people who visit your site to join your email list and receive updates from you. It is recommended to position opt-in forms in highly visible areas of your website, such as the header, sidebar, or footer. You can also capture people's attention and encourage sign-ups by utilizing slide-ins, pop-ups, or exit-intent forms on your website.

Provide Users with Unique Content or Discounts.

As an incentive for people to sign up for your email

list, you can give your email subscribers access to special content or discounts on your products. This may take the form of cost-free resources, e-books, whitepapers, or discounts on various goods and services. Be sure that the offer is both relevant and valuable to the audience you are trying to reach.

Hold competitions and give away prizes.

To encourage sign-ups and grow your email list, a fun and engaging way to encourage sign-ups is to host a contest or giveaway. Check that the prize is appropriate for the audience you're trying to reach and fits in well with your brand. To get the most people to sign up, publicize the contest or giveaway on your website, in your social media accounts, and in your email marketing campaigns.

Drive sign-ups by utilizing various social media platforms.

You can increase the number of people who sign up for your email list by utilizing social media and including links to your sign-up form in your social media profiles and posts. You can also target your audience and encourage sign-ups with the help of advertisements on social media.

Make use of word-of-mouth marketing.

Utilizing your current subscribers as a resource, referral marketing can be an effective strategy for expanding your email list. By providing current subscribers with a discount or other incentive for referring friends or coworkers to your email list, you can encourage them to bring in new subscribers on their own.

Joint venture with other companies or influential people

To expand the size of your email list, consider forming partnerships with other companies or influential people in your sector. Collaborate on the creation of content or promotions that are congruent with both of your brands and provide an incentive for their audience to sign up for your email list as part of the collaboration.

Make use of QR Codes as well as SMS Sign-Ups.

The use of QR codes and text message sign-ups is a cutting-edge method for gaining new email subscribers. You can encourage people to sign up for your mailing list by including a QR code or an SMS sign-up option on your marketing materials, such as flyers or business cards.

Conclusion

Creating an email list that is of a high quality is absolutely necessary if you want your email marketing campaigns to be successful. Creating high-quality lead magnets, optimizing your website for sign-ups, offering exclusive content or discounts, running contests or giveaways, using social media to drive sign-ups, using referral marketing, partnering with other businesses or influencers, and using QR codes or SMS sign-ups are some of the strategies we've discussed in this chapter for capturing and engaging your audience. Other strategies include partnering with other businesses or influencers, using QR codes, and running contests or giveaways. You will be able to expand your email list and make the most of your marketing potential by running efficient email campaigns if you put these strategies into action.

Chapter 3: Crafting Effective Email Content: Writing Strategies to Increase Engagement and Conversion

Creating compelling content for your emails is absolutely necessary if you want your email marketing campaigns to be successful. Your content ought to be compelling, engaging, and specifically crafted for the people who will be reading it. In this chapter, we will discuss writing strategies that can help increase engagement and conversion rates in your email marketing campaigns.

Maintain an interesting and concise subject line in your emails.

Your subscribers' inboxes will initially contain nothing but your subject line when they open your email. To get them to open your email, make sure it is concise, interesting, and compelling all at the same time. To get people's attention, emphasize the sense of urgency, personalize the message, and use language focused on taking action.

Make Your Emails More Personalized

When it comes to engaging your audience and developing a relationship with your subscribers, personalization is absolutely essential. To make your emails more relevant and personalized, use personalization tokens such as the recipient's name or location, for example.

Make use of a call to action that is unmistakable and compelling.

The action that you want your subscribers to take, such as making a purchase or visiting your website, is what is known as your call-to-action, or CTA. Make sure that your call to action stands out in the email and that you encourage people to take action by using language that is both understandable and compelling.

Make a connection with your audience through the use of storytelling.

Storytelling is an effective strategy for connecting with your audience and making your brand seem more approachable to potential customers. Make your emails more engaging and memorable by incorporating narratives that are congruent with your brand and that have meaning for your readership.

Make sure that your content is concise and easy to scan.

Your subscribers are likely to be very busy people who simply do not have the time to read lengthy emails. Utilize headings, bullet points, and short paragraphs to keep the content you've written concise and easy to scan. Your subscribers will have an easier time quickly comprehending your message and acting on it as a result of this.

Utilize Forms of Social Proof to Establish Trust

Building trust with your audience through the use of social proof, such as reviews and testimonials from other customers, is an effective strategy. You can encourage your subscribers to take action by demonstrating the value of your goods or services through the use of social proof in your email communications with them.

Create a Sense of Urgency by Leveraging Fear of Missing Out

Fear of missing out (also known as FOMO) is a powerful motivator that, when applied to your email marketing campaigns, can increase engagement and conversion rates. Use language that creates a sense of urgency and scarcity, such as "limited time offer" or "limited availability." For example, "limited time offer" or "limited availability."

You can optimize your content by using A/B testing.

The use of A/B testing is a powerful tool for optimizing the content of your emails in order to achieve better results. You can improve the efficiency of your campaigns by experimenting with a variety of subject lines, calls to action (CTAs), and content to see which one is most well received by your audience.

Conclusion

Creating compelling content for your emails is absolutely necessary if you want your email marketing campaigns to be successful. In this chapter, we discussed writing strategies that can be used to increase engagement and conversion rates. These strategies include keeping your subject line short and engaging, personalizing your emails, using a clear and compelling call-to-action, using storytelling to connect with your audience, keeping your content short and scannable, using social proof to build trust, using FOMO to create a sense of urgency, and using A/B testing to optimize your content. All of these strategies can be found in this chapter's accompanying chapter handout. By putting these strategies into action, you will be able to produce email content that is not only compelling and engaging but also drives results for your company.

Chapter 4

Chapter 4: Email Design Best Practices: Creating Visually Compelling Emails that Get Results

The design of your emails is one of the most important factors that determines how successful your email marketing campaigns are. Your subscribers' attention can be captured with a visually compelling email, which can also increase engagement and conversion rates. In this chapter, we will discuss best practices for email design in order to create visually compelling emails that are effective in getting results.

Maintain the Straightforwardness and Purity of Your Design.

When it comes to designing emails, keeping things as simple as possible is essential. To direct the attention of your subscribers and make it easy for them to interact with your content, employ a design that is uncluttered, straightforward, and has a distinct hierarchy.

Make Use Of Visuals That Are Eye-Catching

Visuals are an effective strategy for grabbing the attention of your subscribers and making your email more interesting to read. Make your email stand out from the rest in their inbox by including some visually appealing content, such as high-quality images, videos, or GIFs.

Employ a Design That Starts With Mobile.

Because mobile devices are responsible for the opening of the vast majority of emails, it is critical that you design your emails with mobile users in mind. On a mobile screen, you should employ a layout with a single column, large text, and buttons that are simple to tap.

Make Sure Your Brand Is Consistent

Maintaining a consistent brand is essential to gaining the audience's trust and making a name for yourself among them. In order to reinforce the identity of your brand, make sure that the colors, fonts, and logo you use in the design of your emails are consistent.

Make the Most of the White Space Available

The empty space, or white space, between elements in your email design is known as "white space." It is an effective component of design that has the potential to both make your content easier to read and to boost engagement. Make effective use of the white space available in your email to direct the attention of your subscribers and make it more visually appealing.

Make Use of a Definable Hierarchy

It will be much simpler for your subscribers to interact with your content if the design of your email includes a distinct hierarchy. You can better organize your content and direct the attention of your subscribers by making use of headings, subheadings, and bulleted lists.

Use Responsive Design

Your email will look great and be easy to read on any device thanks to responsive design, whether it's a desktop computer, a tablet, or a mobile device. Responsive design ensures this. You can optimize your email for all different screen sizes and boost engagement by using a design that is responsive.

Utilize A/B testing in order to perfect your layout.

A/B testing is a powerful method that can be utilized to optimize the design of your email in order to achieve better results. You can improve the efficiency of your campaigns by experimenting with a variety of design elements, such as colors, images, and layout, to see which ones have the greatest impact on your target audience.

Conclusion

The design of your emails is one of the most important factors in the success of your email marketing campaigns. In this chapter, we have discussed best practices for email design in order to create visually compelling emails that get results. These best practices include keeping your design simple and clean, using eye-catching visuals, using a mobile-first design, using consistent branding, using white space effectively, using a clear hierarchy, using responsive design, and using A/B testing in order to optimize your design. You will be able to craft visually appealing emails that grab the attention of your subscribers, which will in turn drive engagement and conversion for your company when you put these best practices into action.

Chapter 5: Maximizing Deliverability: Ensuring Your Emails Reach Your Subscribers' Inboxes

Deliverability of email refers to the ability of your messages to make it to the inboxes of the people who have subscribed to them. It is essential to the success of your email marketing campaigns that you maximize the percentage of messages that are successfully delivered. In this chapter, we will discuss various strategies that can be used to increase the likelihood that your emails will be received successfully by your subscribers.

Employ the Services of a Reliable Email Service Provider (ESP)

To ensure the highest possible deliverability, it is essential to use a reputable email service provider. Make sure that your emails are not marked as spam by selecting an email service provider (ESP) that has a solid reputation and is acknowledged by internet service providers (ISPs).

Create a Mailing List with Excellent Content

In order to maximize deliverability, it is essential to construct a high-quality email list consisting of engaged subscribers. By regularly validating your email addresses and removing inactive subscribers, you can keep your email list clean and ensure that it is always up to date.

Employ the Practice of Double Opt-In Double opt-in refers to a procedure in which subscribers confirm their email address after signing up for your email list. This process ensures that your subscribers are interested in receiving your emails and reduces the likelihood that your emails will be marked as spam. This process also ensures that your subscribers are interested in receiving your emails.

Make Sure to Stick to a Regular Sending Schedule

Establishing a regular pattern of sending emails to your subscribers on a predetermined schedule can help improve deliverability. This is accomplished through the use of a consistent sending schedule. This can help build trust with internet service providers (ISPs), which can reduce the likelihood that your emails will be marked as spam.

Always keep an eye on your email analytics.

Monitoring your email analytics can assist you in locating deliverability problems and determining what steps need to be taken to rectify them. Make sure that your emails are reaching the inboxes of your subscribers by monitoring the percentage of emails that are opened, the percentage that are clicked through, and the percentage that are bounced.

Segment Your Email List

When you segment your email list, you can send targeted messages to your subscribers that are based on their interests, behaviors, and preferences. This can help improve the deliverability of your emails. This has the potential to help increase engagement as well as reduce the likelihood that your emails will be marked as spam.

Employ a Sender Name and Email Address That Are Easily Recognizable

Building trust with your subscribers is essential to improving deliverability, and using a sender name and email address that are easily recognizable is one way to do so. Make sure that your sender name is either your company name or a name that is easily recognizable, and that you use the same email address for all of your email marketing campaigns.

Implement a Robust Email Authentication System.

Email authentication is a process that helps reduce the likelihood of your emails being labeled as spam by verifying the authenticity of your emails and ensuring that they have not been tampered with. Improve the deliverability of your emails by utilizing a robust email authentication method such as SPF, DKIM, or DMARC.

Conclusion

It is essential to the success of your email marketing campaigns that you maximize the percentage of messages that are successfully delivered. Using a reputable email service provider, building a high-quality email list, employing double opt-in, employing a consistent sending schedule, monitoring your email analytics, segmenting your email list, employing a recognizable sender name and email address, and employing a strong email authentication are some of the strategies we've discussed in this chapter to ensure that your emails reach the inboxes of your subscribers. Other strategies we've covered include using a strong email authentication. You can improve the deliverability of your emails and make certain that they are reaching the inboxes of your subscribers by putting these strategies into action.

Chapter 6

Chapter 6: Segmentation and Personalization: How to Target the Right People with the Right Message

When it comes to your email marketing campaigns, segmentation and personalization are two powerful techniques that can help increase engagement and conversion rates. You can improve the relevance of your emails by targeting the appropriate people with the appropriate message. This will also increase the likelihood that your subscribers will take some sort of action. In this chapter, we will discuss various strategies for segmenting audiences and personalizing communications in order to address the appropriate individuals with the appropriate information.

Segment Your Email List

It is possible to effectively target the appropriate individuals with the appropriate message by segmenting your email list. To send targeted messages that are both relevant and engaging to your subscribers, you should segment your list based on the interests, behaviors, preferences, and demographics of your subscribers.

Utilize Tokens for Personalization

Tokens of personalization, such as your subscribers' names, locations, or previous purchases, are an effective tool for making emails appear more relevant and personalized to the recipient. To boost engagement and conversion rates, incorporate personalization tokens into your subject line, content, and call-to-action statements.

Make use of the dynamic content.

The interests, habits, and preferences of your subscribers can influence the content of your website, and this can lead to the creation of dynamic content. Increase the relevance of your emails and the amount of engagement they receive by using dynamic content, which displays different images, text, or products based on how your subscribers interact with your emails.

Use Triggered Emails

Emails that are sent automatically and depend on the actions or behaviors of your subscribers can be called "triggered emails." Sending out automated emails with personalized messages, such as "welcome" emails, "abandoned cart" emails, or "post-purchase follow-up" emails, can be an effective way to boost customer engagement and conversion rates.

Test with A/B Splits.

A/B testing is a powerful method for optimizing your email marketing campaigns. This method involves testing multiple aspects of an email, such as the subject line, the content, or the images, to determine which one is more appealing to the target audience. You can personalize your messages, increase their relevance, and increase engagement with the help of A/B testing.

Use Retargeting Ads

When a subscriber leaves your website or email campaign, they may be subjected to retargeting ads, which are advertisements that appear on other websites. To increase conversion, you can use retargeting ads to show individuals personalized messages or products based on the level of engagement they have had with your email marketing campaign.

Utilize User Reviews and Opinion Polls

Collecting information about the interests, preferences, and behaviors of your subscribers through the use of feedback and surveys is an effective method. You can increase the personalization of your messages and the relevance and engagement they generate by utilizing feedback and surveys.

Conclusion

When conducting email marketing campaigns, segmentation and personalization are two effective strategies that can be used to target the appropriate audience with the appropriate message. The strategies of segmentation and personalization have been discussed in this chapter. These strategies include: segmenting your email list; making use of personalization tokens; making use of dynamic content; making use of triggered emails; making use of A/B testing; making use of retargeting ads; and making use of feedback and surveys. If you put these strategies into action, you'll be able to boost the relevance and engagement of your email marketing campaigns, which will, in turn, drive results for your company.

Chapter 7: Automation and Drip Campaigns: Streamlining Your Email Marketing Workflow

Your workflow for email marketing can be greatly simplified with the help of powerful tools like automation and drip campaigns, which also help to improve the efficiency and effectiveness of your campaigns. In this chapter, we will discuss automation and drip campaign strategies as a means of streamlining the processes involved in your email marketing.

Make use of automated "welcome" email messages.

As soon as a new subscriber signs up for your email list, they are greeted with a warm and friendly email that is sent automatically. You can introduce your brand, establish expectations, and encourage engagement with your emails all through the use of welcome emails.

Utilize Emails of Abandoned Carts

Emails called "abandoned cart emails" are sent out automatically to subscribers who have left items in their shopping cart but have not completed their purchase. Emails sent to subscribers whose shopping carts have been abandoned can be used to remind them of the items they have in the cart and encourage them to complete their purchase.

Make Use Of Emails For Post-Purchase Follow-Ups

Post-purchase follow-up emails are emails that are sent out automatically to subscribers after a purchase has been made by the subscriber. Follow-up emails sent after a purchase should be used to express gratitude to subscribers for their purchase, provide details about the order, and encourage additional purchases.

Use Drip Campaigns

Drip campaigns are a type of automated campaign that are delivered to subscribers over the course of a predetermined amount of time. You can nurture your subscribers, provide value, and encourage engagement with your brand through the use of drip campaigns.

Make use of personalized content as well as dynamic content.

Increasing the level of engagement with your automated campaigns can be accomplished in powerful ways through the use of personalized and dynamic content. Make use of personalization tokens and dynamic content to craft messages that are specifically catered to the interests, habits, and preferences of your subscribers.

Use Triggers and Segmentation

Personalizing your automated campaigns and increasing their relevance and engagement can be accomplished in powerful ways by utilizing triggers and segmentation. Sending targeted messages to your subscribers based on their actions or interests can be accomplished through the use of triggers and segmentation.

Test with A/B Splits.

A/B testing is a powerful method for optimizing your automated campaigns. This method involves testing different aspects of your campaign, such as the subject line, the content, or the calls-to-action, to determine which one has the greatest impact on your audience.

Conclusion

Your workflow for email marketing can be greatly simplified with the help of powerful tools like automation and drip campaigns, which also help to improve the efficiency and effectiveness of your campaigns. The strategies of automation and drip campaigning have been discussed in this chapter. These strategies include the use of automated welcome emails,

emails for abandoned shopping carts, post-purchase follow-up emails, drip campaigns, personalization and dynamic content, triggers and segmentation, and A/B testing. You'll be able to improve the relevance and engagement of your marketing campaigns, as well as streamline the workflow of your email marketing, if you put these strategies into action.

Chapter 8

Chapter 8: A/B Testing: Optimizing Your Email Campaigns for Maximum Impact

A/B testing is an effective method for optimizing your email marketing campaigns. This method involves testing multiple aspects of an email, such as the subject line, the content, and the calls-to-action, to determine which one has the greatest impact on the recipients. In this chapter, we will discuss various

A/B testing strategies that can be used to improve the effectiveness of your email marketing campaigns.

Determine the Effect of Each Variable Separately

When running A/B tests, it is essential to test one variable at a time in order to properly determine the influence that each variable has on the overall performance of your campaign. This gives you the ability to determine which variable had the most significant influence on the results you obtained.

Determine Your Measures of Success

It is important to define your success metrics before you conduct an A/B test. Some examples of success metrics include open rates, click-through rates, and conversion rates. Because of this, you will be able to measure the impact of your test and determine which version performed better.

Use a Large Sample Size

Your test results will be statistically significant and representative of your entire email list if you use a large sample size. This will ensure that your test is accurate. To determine the appropriate sample size for your test, you can determine it with the help of a sample size calculator.

Conduct tests on both the content and the design.

It is important to test both content and design elements when conducting A/B tests. These elements could include subject lines, headlines, images, or layout. The goal is to determine which of these elements will resonate most strongly with your audience.

Conduct Examinations on a Frequent Basis

Testing your email campaigns with A/B splits on a regular basis is absolutely necessary in order to optimize them for maximum impact. It is important to conduct regular testing of the various aspects of your campaigns to guarantee that you are continuously improving your results.

Utilize Automation in Order to Carry Out A/B Testing

Automating the A/B testing process can help to simplify the testing procedure and make it more straightforward to carry out tests on a more frequent basis. To make the testing process more manageable, make use of an email marketing automation platform that also includes features for A/B testing.

Test Across Different Segments

Testing across different segments of your audience, such as age, location, or interests, can provide you with valuable insights into what will resonate most strongly with each subset of that audience. Utilize segmentation to test out various iterations of your campaigns on a variety of different segments in order to achieve the best possible results.

Conclusion

Testing with the A/B method is an effective strategy for optimizing your email marketing campaigns to achieve the greatest possible impact. Testing one variable at a time, defining your success metrics, using a large sample size, testing both content and design, testing on a regular basis, using automation for A/B testing, and testing across different segments are some of the A/B testing strategies that we covered in this chapter. You will be able to maximize the effectiveness of your email marketing campaigns and generate results for your company if you put these strategies into action.

Chapter 9: Email Metrics and Analytics: Measuring Success and Identifying Areas for Improvement

Metrics and analytics for emails are essential tools for determining how successful your email marketing campaigns have been and locating weak spots that need to be strengthened. In this chapter, we will discuss email metrics and analytics as a means of gauging the level of success achieved and locating areas in which further development is necessary.

Open Rate

The percentage of subscribers who actually opened your email is known as the open rate. If your email's open rate is high, it means that the subject line and sender name you used were compelling and attracted the attention of your subscribers. If your email's open rate is low, it's a good sign that the subject line and sender name could use some work.

Ratio de Click-Throughs

The percentage of subscribers who open your email and click on a link is known as the click-through rate (CTR). Your content and your call to action were compelling and encouraged engagement if you have a high click-through rate, which indicates that they were successful. A low click-through rate is an indication that the content on your website and the call to action need to be improved.

The rate of conversion

The conversion rate is the percentage of subscribers who took the desired action, such as making a purchase or filling out a form, after clicking on a link in one of your emails. Examples of this action include filling out a form or making a purchase. A high conversion rate indicates that your email effectively drove action and that you have achieved the goals you set for this campaign. If your conversion rate is low, it suggests that your email could use some improvements to better motivate recipients to take action.

Rate of Bounce

The percentage of emails that were unable to be delivered and were sent back to the sender is referred to as the bounce rate. A high percentage of undeliverable messages suggests that your email list needs to be cleaned, or that there may be problems with the authentication or sending practices you use for your emails.

Rate of Unsubscription

The percentage of subscribers who remain on your email list after being sent an email and then decide to remove themselves from the list is known as the unsubscribe rate. If your unsubscribe rate is high, it's possible that the content you provide or the frequency at which you provide it is not living up to the standards set by your subscribers.

Earnings From Sales Obtained

The amount of money made through your email marketing campaign is referred to as the "revenue generated." When it comes to calculating the return on investment (ROI) of your email marketing efforts and gauging the overall success of your campaign, this metric is absolutely essential.

Engagement Rate

Your email's overall engagement is measured by its "engagement rate," which takes into account such metrics as opens, clicks, and shares. This metric provides a more comprehensive view of the success of your campaign and can assist in identifying areas in both the content and design of your emails that could use some improvement.

Conclusion

Metrics and analytics for emails are essential tools for determining how successful your email marketing campaigns have been and locating weak spots that need to be strengthened. In this chapter, we covered a variety of email metrics and analytics, such as the open rate, the click-through rate, the conversion rate, the bounce rate, the unsubscribe rate, the revenue generated, and the engagement rate. These metrics and analytics are used to measure success and identify areas for improvement. You will be able to optimize your email marketing campaigns for maximum impact and drive results for your company if you regularly monitor and analyze these metrics.

Chapter 10: Mobile Optimization: Making Your Emails Mobile-Friendly and Responsive

In order for your email marketing campaigns to be successful, mobile optimization is absolutely necessary. Because more and more people are accessing their email on mobile devices, it is critical that your emails are optimized for mobile use and responsive to different screen sizes. In this chapter, we will discuss mobile optimization strategies that will make your emails responsive and mobile-friendly.

Make use of a design that is responsive.

When it comes to making your emails compatible with mobile devices, using a design that is responsive is absolutely necessary. Your email will appear correctly regardless of the screen size of the device on which it is being viewed if it has been designed with a responsive layout. This ensures that the content of your emails can be read and navigated without difficulty on mobile devices.

Maintain a Narrow Width for Your Email

If you keep the width of your email to a minimum, somewhere around 600 pixels, you can ensure that it will display properly on the screen of the vast majority of mobile devices without the user having to zoom in or scroll horizontally.

Make the font size fairly large.

If you want your email to be easily readable on mobile devices, using a large font size is the best way to go. When writing the body text, use a font size of at least 14 pixels, and when writing headlines and calls to action, use a font size of at least 22 pixels.

Make Use of Fonts That Are Easy to Read and Simple

Your email will be easily readable on mobile devices if you use fonts that are straightforward and uncomplicated to read. When working with a small screen, you should avoid using decorative fonts or fonts that are difficult to read.

Make limited use of visuals.

When using mobile devices, where internet speeds may be slower, you can help reduce the amount of time it takes for your email to load by using images sparingly. To ensure that subscribers who have images turned off will still receive the intended message, use alternative text when you upload images.

Employ a layout with a single column.

If you want to make sure that your email can be easily read on mobile devices, use a layout with only one column. Try to avoid using multiple columns or complex layouts, as these things may not display correctly on screens with a smaller resolution.

Make use of calls to action that are unmistakable and compelling.

To ensure that your subscribers can easily take action on your email from their mobile devices, it is important to use calls-to-action that are both clear and compelling. Use buttons or links that have text that is easy to read and that can be clicked on easily on smaller screens.

Conclusion

In order for your email marketing campaigns to be successful, mobile optimization is absolutely necessary. In this chapter, we discussed mobile optimization strategies that can make your emails mobile-friendly and responsive. These strategies include using a responsive design, keeping your email width narrow, using a large font size, using fonts that are simple and easy to read, using images sparingly, using a single column layout, and using clear and compelling calls-to-action. You will be able to guarantee that your emails are simple to read and navigate on mobile devices by putting these strategies into action, and you will also be able to generate results for your company.

Chapter 11: Email List Hygiene: Maintaining a Clean and Active Subscriber List

It is absolutely necessary for the success of your email marketing campaigns to keep an email list that is both up to date and active. Your email deliverability and the effectiveness of your campaigns may suffer if you have subscribers who do not engage with your content or are inactive. In this chapter, we will discuss various email list hygiene strategies that can be used to keep a subscriber list that is both clean and active.

Take Active Subscribers Off the List

Eliminating inactive subscribers, such as those who haven't opened or clicked on any of your emails in a predetermined amount of time, can help improve the engagement with your email campaigns as well as their ability to be delivered. Think about unsubscribing people from your email list who haven't interacted with any of your messages in the past six months to a year.

Keep an eye on the complaint and bounce rates.

Monitoring your email list's complaint and bounce rates can help you identify problems with your email sending practices and your email list. If your email list has a high bounce rate, it may be time to clean it up. On the other hand, if you have a high complaint rate, it may mean that your content or frequency is not living up to the standards that your subscribers have set for you.

Use Double Opt-In

When you use double opt-in, which requires subscribers to confirm their subscription before being added to your email list, you can help ensure that your subscribers are actively engaged with your content and interested in it by making them confirm their subscription. It is possible that the number of inactive or disinterested subscribers that are added to your list will decrease as a result of doing this.

Make it Simple for People to Opt Out

If you make it simple for subscribers to remove themselves from your list, you can help maintain its freshness and activity level. Include a link to unsubscribe in all of your emails, and ensure that the process is easy to understand and follow.

Encourage participation as well as feedback.

You can maintain an active and engaged list of subscribers by encouraging participation and feedback from those on your list of subscribers. Request feedback from your subscribers, conduct surveys, and offer them opportunities to interact with your brand and the content you produce.

Targeting Active Subscribers Through the Use of Segmentation

When you use segmentation to target active subscribers, you can help ensure that your campaigns are communicating with the appropriate individuals at the appropriate time. Sending targeted messages to subscribers who have recently engaged with your content or taken the desired action can be accomplished through the use of segmentation.

Conclusion

It is absolutely necessary for the success of your email marketing campaigns to keep an email list that is both up to date and active. In this chapter, we discussed various email list hygiene strategies that can be used to keep a subscriber list clean and full of active users. These strategies include removing inactive subscribers, monitoring bounce and complaint rates, using double opt-in, ensuring that it is simple to unsubscribe, encouraging engagement and feedback, and using segmentation to target users who are currently logged in. You can ensure that your email list is clean and active by putting these strategies into action. You can also improve the engagement and deliverability of your campaigns, which will ultimately drive results for your company.

Chapter 12: Integration and Cross-Channel Marketing: Combining Email with Social Media, SEO, and More

Integration and marketing across multiple channels are extremely important factors to consider if you want your email marketing campaigns to have the greatest possible impact. You can reach a larger audience and generate more engagement and conversions by combining email with other channels, such as social media, search engine optimization (SEO), and other methods. In this chapter, we will discuss integration and cross-channel marketing strategies with the goal of maximizing the impact of email marketing by combining it with other channels.

Make use of social media platforms in order to expand your email list.

Reaching a larger audience and expanding your subscriber base can be accomplished in a powerful way by growing your email list through the use of social media. You can promote your email list and encourage people to sign up for it by utilizing social media platforms such as Facebook and Twitter.

Email can be used to drive engagement on social media.

By using email as a driver for social media engagement, you can help increase the reach of your social media content and the amount of engagement it receives. In your emails, include links to your social media accounts, and encourage your subscribers to follow or interact with your brand on the various social networks.

Employ Search Engine Optimization to Drive Sign-Ups for Your Email List

Your email list's visibility and reach can be improved if you use search engine optimization (SEO) to drive email sign-ups. To increase traffic and encourage sign-ups, you should make use of targeted keywords and landing pages that have been optimized.

You can increase traffic to your website by using email.

When you use email to direct traffic to your website, you can help increase both the visibility of your website content and the engagement with it. In the emails you send out, include links to relevant content or promotions and encourage your subscribers to check out your website.

Use Personalization to Combine Channels

You can help increase relevance and engagement across channels by using personalization to combine channels, such as by using a subscriber's social media behavior or website activity to personalize your emails. Using personalization to combine channels can be done in a number of different ways.

Retargeting can be used to combine different channels.

By retargeting email subscribers with social media ads or vice versa, for example, you can help increase engagement and conversions by keeping your brand at the forefront of your customers' minds across multiple channels by using retargeting to combine channels.

Conclusion

Integration and marketing across multiple channels are extremely important factors to consider if you want your email marketing campaigns to have the greatest possible impact. In this chapter, we discussed integration and cross-channel marketing strategies to combine email with other channels for maximum impact. These strategies include utilizing social media to grow your email list, utilizing email to drive social media engagement, utilizing SEO to drive email sign-ups, utilizing email to drive traffic to your website, utilizing personalization and retargeting to combine channels, and utilizing retargeting and personalization to combine channels. You can expand the reach, engagement, and conversions of your email marketing campaigns and drive results for your company if you put these strategies into action.

Chapter 13: Lead Magnets and Opt-Ins: Strategies for Encouraging Subscriber Sign-Ups

In order to construct a robust subscriber base and propel the success of your email marketing campaigns, it is essential to encourage subscribers to sign up for your email list. In this chapter, we will discuss lead magnets and opt-in strategies to increase the number of people who sign up to become subscribers.

Make use of a lead magnet.

By offering something of value to subscribers and highlighting your status as an industry expert through the distribution of a lead magnet, such as a free e-book, webinar, or white paper, you can encourage them to sign up for your email list. To get more people to sign up for your service, you should publicize your lead magnet on your website, in social media, and through any other channels you use.

Forms for opting in should be used on your website.

When you use opt-in forms on your website, whether they are pop-ups or embedded forms, you can encourage visitors to sign up for your email list by making it simple and convenient for them to do so. Make your opt-in forms stand out from the crowd by giving them compelling copy and design to use. This will encourage people to sign up.

Make available a Welcome Series

New subscribers can be encouraged to engage with your brand and remain subscribed to your email list by providing a welcome series. This can take the form of a series of introductory emails or a special offer that is only available to new subscribers.

Make use of social evidence.

You can demonstrate the value of your email list to prospective subscribers by using social proof, such as customer testimonials or a high subscriber count. This will encourage them to sign up for your email list.

Provide access to exclusive content as well as special offers.

It is possible to encourage subscribers to sign up for your email list by providing value to them in the form of exclusive content or promotions, such as discounts or early access to new products. This can be done by demonstrating the unique offerings that your brand has to offer.

Make sure you have a distinct call to action.

By making it obvious to site visitors what steps they need to take in order to sign up for your email list, which can be accomplished by using a call-to-action statement such as "Subscribe now" or "Join our email list," you can increase the number of people who do so.

Conclusion

In order to construct a robust subscriber base and propel the success of your email marketing campaigns, it is essential to encourage subscribers to sign up for your email list. In this chapter, we discussed lead magnets and opt-in strategies to encourage subscriber sign-ups. These strategies include utilizing a lead magnet, utilizing opt-in forms on your website, providing a welcome series, utilizing social proof, providing exclusive content or promotions, and utilizing a clear call-to-action. You can increase the number of subscribers on your email list as well as the quality of those subscribers, which will drive results for your company if you implement these strategies.

Chapter 14: Emails for E-commerce: Strategies to Drive Sales and Increase Revenue

E-commerce companies have access to a powerful tool in the form of email marketing, which they can use to drive sales and boost revenue. In this chapter, we will explore email strategies specifically tailored to e-commerce businesses in order to drive sales and increase revenue. These strategies will be specifically tailored to e-commerce businesses.

Emails for Abandoned Shopping Carts

Emails sent to customers whose shopping carts have been abandoned are an effective method for recovering sales that have been lost. These emails remind customers of the items they have in their carts and encourage them to complete their purchase. You can increase the effectiveness of your emails to customers who have abandoned their shopping carts by including compelling copy and design, as well as making personalized product recommendations.

Emails Confirming Orders and Providing Receipts

Emails confirming orders and providing receipts offer a window of opportunity to upsell or cross-sell related products and encourage repeat purchases. Enhance the efficiency of your order confirmation and receipt emails by including personalized product recommendations, in addition to using copy and design that are compelling to the reader.

Emails Suggesting Other Products to Purchase

Product recommendation emails can help drive sales and increase revenue by suggesting relevant products that may be of interest to the recipient. These emails are based on a customer's purchase history or browsing behavior, which the customer has provided. Increase the efficiency of your product recommendation emails by including compelling copy and design, in addition to providing customers with personalized product recommendations.

Emails with promotional content

By offering customers an incentive to make a

purchase, promotional emails, such as those advertising sales or special offers, can help drive sales and
increase revenue for a business. To make your promotional emails more effective, you should use copy and
design that are compelling, as well as clear calls to
action and deadlines.

Recovering Lost Emails

Re-engaging customers and encouraging them to
make additional purchases can be facilitated through
the use of "win-back" emails, which are sent to clients
who have not made a purchase for a predetermined
amount of time. The efficiency of your "win-back"
emails can be improved by including personalized
product recommendations or special offers, as well
as using copy and design that are compelling to the
reader.

Emails sent after a purchase for follow-up purposes

It is possible to increase customer loyalty and encourage repeat purchases by sending follow-up emails
after a customer has made a purchase. These emails
should express gratitude for the customer's purchase
and encourage them to provide feedback or reviews.
To make your post-purchase follow-up emails more
effective, you should use copy and design that are
compelling, as well as clear calls to action and incentives for providing feedback or reviews.

Conclusion

E-commerce companies have access to a powerful
tool in the form of email marketing, which they can
use to drive sales and boost revenue. Email strategies

that are specifically tailored to e-commerce businesses in order to drive sales and increase revenue have been discussed in this chapter. These strategies include emails sent to customers whose shopping carts were abandoned, emails confirming and acknowledging orders, emails recommending products, promotional emails, win-back emails, and post-purchase follow-up emails. You will be able to increase the effectiveness of your email marketing campaigns and drive results for your e-commerce business if you implement these strategies and put them into action.

Chapter 15: Event and Product Launch Emails: Creating Buzz and Driving Engagement

Email marketing is a potent instrument that can be used to generate excitement and interest in upcoming events as well as product launches. In this chapter, we will discuss email strategies that are specifically tailored to events and product launches in order to generate excitement and encourage engagement with the audience.

Emails requesting a "Save the Date"

Emails that ask recipients to "save the date" are an effective method for announcing an upcoming event or product launch and building anticipation among your audience. To make your emails reminding people to save the date more effective, you should use copy and design that are compelling, provide clear details, and include calls to action.

Invitation Emails

Email invitations sent to a particular group of people or to VIPs can contribute to the creation of an intimate and individualized atmosphere surrounding the launch of your event or product. To make your invitation emails more effective, use personalized copy and design, in addition to providing clear details and calls-to-action.

Reminder Emails

Sending reminder emails to your audience closer to the date of the event or product launch can help ensure that they don't forget about the event or launch and can encourage them to take action. To make your reminder emails more effective, use copy and design that is compelling, provide clear details, and include calls to action.

Sneak Peek Emails

Sending your audience emails with sneak peek images that give them a first look at the event or product can help generate excitement and anticipation among that audience. In order to make your sneak peek emails more effective, you should use copy and design that are compelling, provide clear details, and include calls to action.

Emails Serving as Follow-Ups

Sending follow-up emails after an event or product launch can be a helpful way to continue the engagement and encourage post-event or post-launch action, such as making purchases or signing up for newsletters. The efficiency of your follow-up emails can be improved by including compelling copy and design, as well as specific details and calls to action.

Emails of appreciation

Sending out "thank you" emails to attendees or customers as a way of expressing appreciation for their participation or purchase can help increase customer loyalty and encourage repeat purchases. To make your thank-you emails more effective, use compelling copy and design, in addition to providing clear details and calls to action.

Conclusion

Email marketing is a potent instrument that can be used to generate excitement and interest in upcoming events as well as product launches. Email strategies that are specifically tailored to events and product launches have been discussed in this chapter. These strategies include save-the-date emails, invitation emails, reminder emails, sneak peek emails, follow-up emails, and thank you emails. The overall goal of these strategies is to generate excitement and encourage engagement. You will be able to increase the effectiveness of your email marketing campaigns and drive results for your event or product launch if you implement these strategies and put them into practice.

Chapter 16: Seasonal and Holiday Emails: Tips and Strategies for Holiday-Themed Campaigns

Email marketing campaigns with a seasonal or holiday focus can be an effective way to connect with your audience and boost engagement and sales during peak times of the year, such as the holiday season and the winter season. In this chapter, we will discuss some helpful hints and techniques for putting together holiday and seasonal email marketing campaigns that are successful.

Prepare for the future.

Email marketing campaigns with a seasonal or holiday focus require careful advance planning in order to be successful. Take into account the timing of your campaigns as well as the messaging, and then plan the content and design of your website accordingly. To evaluate the success of your campaigns, you should first establish goals and then keep track of the results.

Make use of imagery and messaging related to the seasons and holidays.

By using imagery and messaging related to seasonal and holiday events, you can help create an experience that is festive and engaging for your subscribers. Make use of colors, graphics, and messaging that are relevant to the season or holiday in order to capture its spirit.

Provide Customers with Unique Discounts and Special Promotions

By incentivizing subscribers to make a purchase and increasing sales during peak times of the year, businesses can capitalize on the benefits of offering exclusive discounts and promotions. Encourage your subscribers to take advantage of your promotions by providing them with distinct calls to action and firm deadlines.

Utilize Personalization and Segmentation to Improve Results

Making use of personalization and segmentation can be of assistance in ensuring that your marketing campaigns are communicating effectively with the intended audience. Make use of subscriber data, such as past purchase history or browsing behavior, to personalize your campaigns and segment your audience for maximum impact. This will allow you to achieve your goals more effectively.

Make Use Of A Joyous Subject Line

By using a subject line that is festive, you can help increase the number of people who open your emails and capture the attention of your subscribers. Make use of the appropriate keywords and messaging to instill a sense of both urgency and excitement in your audience.

Consider Mobile Optimization

Your seasonal and holiday-themed email marketing campaigns cannot be successful without mobile optimization being taken into consideration. Make sure that your emails are optimized for mobile devices by using a design that is responsive and clear calls to action.

Conclusion

Email marketing campaigns with a seasonal or holiday focus can be an effective way to connect with your audience and boost engagement and sales during peak times of the year, such as the holiday season and the winter season. In this chapter, we covered some helpful hints and pointers for creating successful seasonal and holiday-themed email marketing campaigns.

Some of the topics covered included: planning ahead, utilizing seasonal and holiday imagery and messaging, offering exclusive promotions and discounts, utilizing personalization and segmentation, utilizing a festive subject line, and considering mobile optimization. You will be able to generate results for your company by creating email campaigns with a seasonal or holiday theme that are both engaging and effective if you put these strategies into action.

Chapter 17: Welcome and Onboarding Emails: Building Strong Relationships with New Subscribers

It is essential to send welcome and onboarding emails to new subscribers in order to build strong relationships with them, as well as to increase engagement and conversions. In this chapter, we will discuss best practices for writing welcome and onboarding emails that are both efficient and effective.

Thank you for the welcome email

The initial email that is sent to a new subscriber is referred to as a "welcome email," and its purpose is to "set the tone for the rest of the relationship." Employ a tone that is warm and inviting, and be sure to provide readers with specific information about what they can anticipate receiving from your email list.

Your Company's Introduction to the Market

New subscribers can benefit from having an understanding of what your brand is all about and why they should care if they are given an introduction to your brand. When introducing your brand to new subscribers, use copy and design that is compelling along with a value proposition that is straightforward.

Onboarding Series

An onboarding series is a series of emails that are sent to new subscribers to introduce them to your brand, educate them about the products or services you offer, and encourage engagement and conversions from the new subscribers. When walking new subscribers through the onboarding process, it is helpful to use a clear and logical sequence of emails, each of which includes clear calls-to-action and deadlines.

Individualization based on categorization

By employing personalization and segmentation, you can increase the likelihood that your welcome and onboarding emails will be read by the appropriate individuals and contain the appropriate information. Personalizing your emails and segmenting your audience so that you can have the greatest possible impact requires using subscriber data, such as location or previous purchase history.

Direct invitations to take action

It is possible to encourage engagement and conversions among new subscribers by using clear calls-to-action, which can help guide new subscribers through the onboarding process. To ensure that your calls to action are noticed, it is important to employ compelling copy and design, in addition to providing clear details and deadlines.

Responses and Opinion Polls

The use of feedback and surveys can help new subscribers feel heard and valued, and they can provide valuable insights that can be used to improve your email list as well as your products and services. To encourage both feedback and survey participation, it is helpful to ask questions that are both clear and succinct, and to also offer a reward for taking part.

Conclusion

It is essential to send welcome and onboarding emails to new subscribers in order to build strong relationships with them, as well as to increase engagement and conversions. Using a welcome email, introducing your brand, using an onboarding series, personalization and segmentation, clear calls-to-action, and feedback and surveys are some of the strategies that we covered in this chapter for creating effective welcome and onboarding emails. You'll be able to create welcome and onboarding emails that are engaging and effective by implementing these strategies, and you'll also be able to build strong relationships with your new subscribers.

Chapter 18: Re-engagement and Win-Back Emails: Bringing Back Inactive Subscribers

Re-engagement and win-back emails can help bring inactive subscribers back into the fold, which can be an important gain for your email marketing campaigns. Inactive subscribers can be a significant loss. In this chapter, we will discuss strategies for efficiently re-engaging previous customers and winning them back as new customers.

Locate the Subscribers Who Are Not Active.

It is essential to identify subscribers who have not been active in order to effectively create re-engagement and win-back emails. Identifying subscribers who haven't interacted with your emails in a predetermined amount of time can be accomplished with the help of data on subscribers, such as open and click-through rates.

Make Use Of Copy That Is Captivating And Design

It is possible to attract the attention of inactive subscribers and encourage them to engage with your emails by using design and copy that are compelling. In order to make your emails stand out from the crowd, use a message that is direct and to the point, along with a design that is captivating.

Provide a Particularly Appealing Promotion or Incentive

Inactive subscribers can be motivated to engage with your emails and make a purchase if you offer a special promotion or incentive. This can help boost your open and click-through rates. Encourage your subscribers to take advantage of your promotions by providing them with distinct calls to action and firm deadlines.

Utilize Personalization and Segmentation to Improve Results

When you use personalization and segmentation, you can increase the likelihood that your re-engagement and win-back emails will be received by the appropriate individuals and convey the intended message. Utilize subscriber data, such as past purchase history or browsing behavior, to personalize your emails and segment your audience for maximum impact. This will allow you to reach more people with your message.

Make sure you have a distinct call to action.

By utilizing a distinct call-to-action, you can assist inactive subscribers in becoming more engaged with your email communications. To make it easy for subscribers to take action, you should use copy and design that are compelling, along with a call to action that is clear and to the point.

Make Use of a Number of Separate Emails

Through the use of a series of emails, you can help guide subscribers who have become inactive in their interaction with your emails over time. To encourage subscribers to take action, you can send them an email series that is organized in a way that is both clear and logical, and that features rising levels of urgency and incentives.

Conclusion

It is essential to send re-engagement and win-back emails in order to bring inactive subscribers back into the fold, as well as to increase engagement and conversions. In this chapter, we discussed some of the strategies that can be used to create effective re-engagement and win-back emails. These strategies include identifying inactive subscribers, utilizing compelling copy and design, providing a unique promotion or incentive, utilizing personalization and

segmentation, utilizing a clear call-to-action, and utilizing a series of emails. You can bring inactive subscribers back into engagement with your email list
and drive results for your company by implementing
these strategies and putting them into practice.

Chapter 19: Email Compliance: Understanding Laws and Regulations for Email Marketing

Email marketing is subject to a number of laws and regulations, and it is essential for companies to understand these regulations and comply with them in order to avoid legal issues and keep a positive reputation. In this chapter, we will discuss the laws and regulations that pertain to email marketing, as well as the strategies that can be utilized to ensure compliance with these requirements.

The CAN-SPAM Act.

The CAN-SPAM Act is a piece of legislation that was passed in the United States with the intention of regulating commercial email messages. Some of the requirements of this legislation include opt-out mechanisms, clear identification of the sender, and accurate subject lines. It is essential for companies to ensure they are in compliance with the CAN-SPAM Act in order to stay out of legal trouble and preserve their good name.

GDPR

The General Data Protection Regulation (GDPR) is a law that was passed by the European Union that establishes guidelines for the gathering and processing of individuals' personal data. It requires companies to obtain explicit consent for the collection and use of personal data, and it gives individuals the right to access and delete their personal data. It also requires businesses to obtain explicit consent for the collection and use of personal data. To stay out of legal hot water and to keep up a good reputation, it is essential for businesses to comply with the General Data Protection Regulation (GDPR).

CASL

The Canadian Anti-Spam Legislation (CASL) is a piece of legislation that was passed in Canada with the intention of regulating commercial email messages. These regulations include mandates for opt-in mechanisms and explicit sender identification. Businesses have a responsibility to ensure that they are in compliance with CASL in order to protect their good names and stay out of legal trouble.

Mechanisms for Opting Out of Emails

A number of laws and regulations governing email marketing, such as the CAN-SPAM Act and CASL, stipulate that an unsubscribe mechanism must be made available to customers. For the sake of avoiding potential legal complications and preserving a positive reputation, it is essential for companies to ensure that it is simple for subscribers to remove themselves from the company's email list.

Protection of Information and Safety of Data

To remain in compliance with the laws and regulations governing email marketing, it is essential to safeguard the data of subscribers and guarantee their data's safety. For the purpose of avoiding legal issues and preserving a positive reputation, it is essential for companies to have transparent policies and procedures in place for the collection, storage, and processing of subscriber data.

Conducting Policy and Procedure Audits and Keeping Them Current Regularly

It is important for businesses to regularly review and update their policies and procedures for maintaining compliance with laws and regulations pertaining to email marketing. This helps to ensure that businesses are aware of any changes that occur in these areas. It is essential for companies to maintain a current awareness of any changes that have been made to the relevant laws and regulations, as well as to modify their internal policies and practices as appropriate.

Conclusion

Email marketing is subject to a number of laws and regulations, and it is essential for companies to understand these regulations and comply with them in order to avoid legal issues and keep a positive reputation. In this chapter, we have discussed the laws and regulations that pertain to email marketing, as well as the strategies that can be utilized to ensure compliance. These strategies include adhering to the CAN-SPAM Act, GDPR, and CASL, providing an unsubscribe mechanism, protecting subscriber data and ensuring that it is secure, and conducting regular reviews and updates of policies and procedures. Businesses can ensure their compliance with the laws and regulations governing email marketing and maintain a positive reputation by putting these strategies into action.

Chapter 20: The Future of Email Marketing: Trends and Predictions for the Next Decade

Email marketing has undergone significant changes over the past decade, and it is likely that the next decade will bring even more changes and innovations than the previous decade did. In this chapter, we will discuss some current trends in email marketing as well as some predictions for the industry's future.

Increased Customization and Automation are Being Employed

Email marketing is likely going to become even more automated and personalized as machine learning and artificial intelligence continue to make strides forward. This will make it possible for companies to create campaigns that are highly targeted and customized, increasing the likelihood that they will resonate with individual subscribers.

Emails that are more interactive and interesting to read.

The future of email marketing is likely to see an increase in the prevalence of emails that are interactive and engaging through the use of gamification and video content, for example. These kinds of emails have the potential to help increase subscriber engagement and maintain their interest in the content you provide.

More Mobile Optimization

Email marketing has been experiencing a trend toward mobile optimization for the past few years, and it is likely that this trend will become even more important in the future. To maximize user engagement and conversions, businesses will need to ensure that the emails they send are compatible with mobile devices as the number of people accessing their email on mobile devices continues to rise.

Maintaining a Strong Focus on the Protection of Personal Information and Data

Email marketers should expect data privacy and

security to continue to be one of their primary areas of focus in the years to come. Businesses will need to ensure that they are complying with these regulations and taking steps to protect subscriber data and ensure that it is secure as laws and regulations continue to develop. This is because businesses will be held responsible for any violations of these laws and regulations.

Integration with Other Distribution Methods for Marketing

Integration with other marketing channels, such as social media and search engine optimization (SEO), is likely to become an even more important aspect of email marketing in the future. Because of this, companies will be able to create marketing campaigns that are more cohesive and integrated, and which can reach subscribers through a variety of channels.

Increased Emphasis on the Quality of the Consumer Experience

In the future of email marketing, it is likely that an even greater emphasis will be placed on the quality of the customer experience. From the moment a customer signs up as a subscriber to the time they make their first purchase, businesses will need to concentrate on developing streamlined and interesting experiences for their customers.

Conclusion

There is a good chance that the future of email marketing will bring even more changes and innovations, such as increased personalization and automation, more interactive and engaging emails, increased mobile optimization, a continued emphasis on data privacy and security, integration with other marketing channels, and an increased focus on the customer experience. Businesses are able to stay ahead of the curve and create effective email marketing campaigns that drive results for their business if they remain current with these trends and predictions and do their best to stay abreast of them.